Soul Shakers

★ SOUL SHAKERS ★

Inspiring Stories from a Presidential Speechwriter

JAMES C. HUMES

DIMENSIONS
FOR LIVING

SOUL SHAKERS
INSPIRING STORIES FROM A PRESIDENTIAL SPEECHWRITER

Copyright © 2007 by James C. Humes

This book is printed on acid-free paper.

Library of Congress Cataloging-in-Publication Data

Humes, James C.
   Soul shakers: inspiring stories from a presidential speechwriter / James C. Humes.
      p.   cm.
Includes indexes.
ISBN-13: 978-0-687-49125-4 (binding: pbk., adhesive, perfect : alk. paper)
1. Christian life—Anecdotes.   2. Spirituality—Anecdotes.   I. Title.
BV4517.H86   2007
242—dc22

                                                           2006036822

07 08 09 10 11 12 13 14 15 16—10 9 8 7 6 5 4 3 2 1

MANUFACTURED IN THE UNITED STATES OF AMERICA

To the Honorable Donald W. Whitehead,
former Federal Chairman
U.S. Appalachian Regional Commission,
who late in his life committed himself to the Lord
and who just before his death urged me
to write this book to inspire others

CONTENTS

Acknowledgments

I owe much to my family for my love of the Bible and American history. My aunt Margaret Humes Collins made me, and later my daughters, Mary and Rachel, learn to recite by memory the books of the Bible and selected psalms. Her mother, my grandmother, Jessica Prindle (Humes) Krom, leader in the D.A.R. and Colonial Dames, instilled in me an interest in American history.

I also want to mention Theresa Vital, a daily Bible reader who provides spiritual input to my four grandchildren.

Introduction

"My Goppy wrote on the moon."

These words by my grandson James to a classmate embarrassed me, but in a sense they were true. As a White House speechwriter for Richard Nixon, I drafted the words for the plaque that was left on the L.E.M. vehicle as part of the Apollo 11 mission. ("Here men from the planet Earth first set foot upon the moon in July 1969 A.D. We came in peace for all mankind.")

As a writer for several presidents, I was called upon for a variety of tasks: the inscription for Duke Ellington's Medal of Freedom ("In the royalty of music no one stands taller or swings higher than the Duke"), a state dinner toast to the visiting king of Thailand, or Rose Garden remarks to the Teacher of the Year.

One writer for Lyndon Johnson, who thought his talents could be better employed in novels than in presidential policy statements, quit the job, saying he was tired of writing "Rose Garden rubbish." His name was Peter Benchley, and the book he wrote was *Jaws*. Yet I felt no such debasement in penning ceremonial remarks. After all, the Gettysburg Address was such a talk! Anyway, if one was asked to write a toast for a visiting head of state, one was allowed to attend the dinner—not to sit down, mind you—but to mingle afterwards during the coffee hour.

When I give my talk around the country, "Confessions of a

White House Writer" (also the title of my autobiography), the first question I am invariably asked is how I got the job. Others might have been chosen for their felicity of phrase, but I was drafted for my fund of anecdotes, vignettes, and quotations. President Nixon once introduced me to his Postmaster General Winton Blount as my "Quotes Master General." When I was assisting President Gerald Ford in writing his memoirs, he asked me to suggest a title, and I gave him "A Time to Heal," from Ecclesiastes.

My White House speechwriting colleague William Safire, in his book *Before the Fall,* quotes President Nixon as saying, "Why can't the rest of you come up with those parables like Jamie Humes?" Nixon liked my offering up historical anecdotes for his Oval Office presentations or Rose Garden remarks because by remembering the gist of the anecdote he could then spin off on it without having to memorize or read two or three paragraphs. For example, when an ambassador retired, Nixon offered a quote I gave him from Thomas Jefferson. Jefferson had arrived in France to become the U.S. ambassador, and the French prime minister asked, "Monsieur Jefferson, have you come to replace Dr. Franklin?" Replied Jefferson, "No one could ever replace Benjamin Franklin; I am only succeeding him."

For my book *The Sir Winston Method* I used as my source Churchill's notes on speech preparation—never published—made in 1900. In those notes, Churchill observed that Jesus never employed the word "salvation." That was a Greek word that the Greek-speaking Paul brought to the Bible. Jesus was preaching to illiterate shepherds and fishermen, to whom such a theological term would have been like describing the task of roping and branding to cowboys as "synergy." Jesus, like many good speakers, avoided fancy words and instead used the Talmudic or rabbinical technique of examples and stories, as in his story of a young man who after wining, womanizing, and wasting his life said, in so many words, "Dad, give me a second chance."

I began amassing my arsenal of anecdotes early, when at age twelve I started to write down inspirational tales from sermons at the First Presbyterian Church of Williamsport, Pennsylvania. I added to my file poignant vignettes from biographies. At age five I sat on the lap of Carl Sandburg when he stayed at our house in Williamsport, where he was giving a lecture. He enchanted me with stories about Lincoln as a boy and made me promise that I would one day read his four-volume work on this most soulful of our presidents.

When in Great Britain in 1953 as an English-Speaking Union Scholar, I met Prime Minister Winston Churchill. He told me, "Young man, study history—in history lie all the secrets of statecraft." I followed his advice by gleaning from biographies incidents in heroic lives that reveal greatness in humanity and character. (I also went on to author five books on Churchill, for which, along with my biography of Shakespeare, Queen Elizabeth II would award me the Order of the British Empire in 1994.)

I gave the name "soul shakers" to my growing collection of anecdotes, and I often used them to close my own talks on an inspirational high note. As a one-time Pennsylvania legislator (I was the youngest at age twenty-eight in 1962), and as the head of the Philadelphia Bar Association, and later as a roving diplomat for the U.S. State Department, I discovered that the word pictures painted in anecdotes are the best way to etch in listeners' minds such abstract virtues as sacrifice, commitment, tolerance, magnanimity, redemption, and love.

My talks on the lecture circuit have carried me to fifty states and twenty-three countries. Any success I have enjoyed as a visiting speaker, trial lawyer, university professor, or even as a lay preacher, I owe to my soul shakers.

My file first came to the attention of Vice President Nixon when I wrote some remarks for President Eisenhower in 1960 at the suggestion of the Reverend Fred Fox, a speechwriter for "the General" (as he liked to be called). I had taught Sunday school for him at the Congregational Church in Williamstown, Massachusetts, when I was attending Williams College. (Fox would later write a history of Protestant hymns.)

As readers of these soul shakers might infer, some of my most poignant stories came out of my direct experience with figures of history such as Presidents Eisenhower, Nixon, Ford, Reagan, and Prime Minister Margaret Thatcher. One story was told to me by the nonagenerian Alice Roosevelt Longworth, daughter of Teddy Roosevelt, who described to me the only time Churchill met her father, in 1900. She told me that her father, then the governor of New York, said to the twenty-six-year-old Churchill, who had just been elected to the House of Commons: "Winston, dare to live your dreams."

In 1969, another child of a president, John Eisenhower, told me in Walter Reed Hospital what his father had just told him, remarks by the old soldier that proved to be his dying words: "Tell them, Johnny, I always loved my wife, I always loved my family, I always loved my country, I always loved my God."

Godspeed and good reading! I hope these soul shakers are as inspirational to you as they have been to me.

SOUL SHAKERS

Rosa the Resolute

Rosa Parks, the woman who made history by deciding to ride in the front of a Birmingham bus, died in 2006. A state funeral was held at the Capitol in Washington, and the president and two former presidents attended. But in all likelihood she would not have approved of all the pomp and circumstance.

Parks was a simple woman, a seamstress by trade. Her clients were three or four wealthy African American women who could not enter a department store or fashionable shop because of their color. So they would point out a dress or gown in *Vogue* or some other fashion magazine, and Parks would copy it with the materials given to her.

One of these women, whose husband owned a chain of "colored hotels," later confided that she was surprised that Parks was the one to break the law and go to jail for doing so, because Parks had always kept to herself, reading the Bible at her lunch breaks.

One day after work, a weary Rosa Parks, taking the bus to her home, decided that enough was enough and sat at the front of the bus, refusing to move back.

Later she told one of her clients that it was time.

A time to tear, and a time to sew;
a time to keep silence, and a time to speak.
                                        —Ecclesiastes 3:7 NRSV

REAGAN'S REQUEST

After the death of Ronald Reagan, it surfaced that the former president had made inquiries at St. Elizabeth Hospital, where John Hinckley was imprisoned. Reagan wanted to know if he could meet with the man who had tried to kill him. Reagan predicated his request on the assurance that it would not disturb Hinckley or complicate his mental condition. Reagan was not encouraged by the prison psychiatrists to make such a visit.

Reagan wanted to let Hinckley know he forgave him. Just days after Reagan was shot, he had told his pastor at George Washington Hospital, "The sooner in my heart I can truly forgive Hinckley, the sooner I will heal."

"You have heard that it was said, 'You shall love your neighbor and hate your enemy.' But I say to you, Love your enemies and pray for those who persecute you."—Matthew 5:43-44 NRSV

APOSTLE TO THE POOR

An Albanian nun in India tried to stop a dying woman from being cast from a hospital, saying, "No one should die alone and unloved."

So she found a temple of a Hindu goddess that was being used for visiting travelers. She turned it into a new home, calling it "the Place of the Immaculate Heart."

Some tough young men of Calcutta tried to stop her by threatening to kill her if she did not leave.

The woman we now know as Mother Teresa replied, "If you kill me, I will just get to heaven sooner." This was the beginning of her new order, the Missionaries of Charity, who vowed to serve the poorest of the poor.

The king will answer them, "Truly I tell you, just as you did it to one of the least of these who are members of my family, you did it to me."—Matthew 25:40 NRSV

To Err Is Human, to Forgive Divine

At an official reception during the Civil War, President Lincoln made a brief speech in which he referred to the Confederates as "erring human beings."

Someone in the audience objected, pointing out that the Confederates were sworn enemies of the Union and asking how Lincoln planned to deal with them.

Lincoln responded, "I am going to destroy them. I am going to make them my friends."

Love your enemies, do good, and lend, expecting nothing in return. Your reward will be great, and you will be children of the Most High; for he is kind to the ungrateful and the wicked.
—Luke 6:35 NRSV

The Syrian Sage

There is a story told in Syria of an old wise man who lived in a cave on a mountaintop outside Damascus. It is said that he could answer any riddle of life. One day, a young boy told his friends that he was going to play a trick on the old man. "I will capture a bird, hold it cupped in my hands, and then ask whether it is dead or alive. If he says 'dead,' I'll let it fly away. If he says 'alive,' I will crush it before opening my hands."

With the cupped bird, the boy went to the cave. Outside its entrance, he yelled, "O wise man, I have a bird in my hands. Is it dead or alive?"

The old man replied, "Lad, the answer is in your hands."

Every one of us shall give account of himself to God.
—Romans 14:12

STEPPING STONES

When Brooklyn Dodger owner Branch Rickey wanted to break the all-white ranks of major league baseball, he recruited Jackie Robinson from the Negro Baseball League. Robinson, an all-American football player from UCLA, had been an officer in World War II and then a star infielder for the Kansas City Monarchs, a Negro League team.

Rickey told Robinson, "I know what you can do with your bat and glove. It's your head that I'm concerned with. . . . You are going to be taunted by some in the stands, and some rival players will call you every four-letter word that is not in the dictionary."

Jackie Robinson withstood racist taunts and murder threats to become the first African American in the Hall of Fame. As Jesse Jackson said at Robinson's funeral, "He made his stumbling blocks into stepping stones."

The Lord shall deliver me from every evil work, and will preserve me unto his heavenly kingdom: to whom be glory for ever and ever. Amen. —2 Timothy 4:18

No Time Like Today

Shortly after his installation in 1958, Pope John XXIII gave word that he wanted to hold a Vatican Council to bring new reform to the church. An ecclesiastical counselor advised Pope John of the tremendous difficulties in organizing such a conference and said it would be impossible to hold a council in 1963. The pope responded that, in that case, the council would begin in 1962.

And it did.

Be not conformed to this world: but be ye transformed by the renewing of your mind, that ye may prove what is that good, and acceptable, and perfect, will of God. —Romans 12:2

PITCHER OR PRESIDENT

In 1960, President Eisenhower greeted in the Oval Office two co-captains of a recent Little League World Series in Williamsport, Pennsylvania. He told the young players a true story of two Kansas boys who dreamed of greatness.

Eisenhower told them about a blond-haired boy and a dark-haired boy. The first boy asked the second boy what he wanted to be when he grew up. "President of the United States of America," was the reply. "What do you want to be?"

"Pitcher for the New York Yankees," answered the first boy.

President Eisenhower was one of those two boys. He told the Little Leaguers the great thing about America was that they could grow up to be anything they wanted to be. The boy who wanted to become president became president of a different sort—president of Abilene Dairy. And President Eisenhower did not achieve his dream.

With many dreams come vanities and a multitude of words.
—Ecclesiastes 5:7 NRSV

STANTON STANDS UP

Elizabeth Cady Stanton became a staunch abolitionist in 1840 at age twenty-five, at a time when abolitionists were considered radical agitators. Eight years later she championed a cause that was in some ways more radical than emancipation of slaves. The cause was women's rights.

At a women's rights convention in July 1848, in Seneca Falls, New York, Stanton made her first speech. "We hold these truths to be self-evident that all men and women are created equal," and she repeated Jefferson's paragraph in the Declaration.

She added, "The history of mankind is a history of repeated injuries and usurpation in the part of man toward woman, having in direct object the establishment of tyranny over her."

This was the first demand for woman suffrage in the United States, made through the vision and courage and determination of Elizabeth Cady Stanton.

At that time Deborah, a prophetess, wife of Lappidoth, was judging Israel. She used to sit under the palm of Deborah between Ramah and Bethel in the hill country of Ephraim; and the Israelites came up to her for judgment.—Judges 4:4-5 NRSV

27

HAMMARSKJÖLD'S HIGHWAY

In 1961, one of the world's noblest public servants, United Nations Secretary-General Dag Hammarskjöld, died in a plane crash on a UN peace mission in Africa. There was some indication of foul play.

In his journal, later published as the book *Markings*, he wrote a prayer asking for a pure heart, a humble heart, a loving heart, a believing heart.

On the last page of his diary he wrote: "In our time the road to holiness leads into and through the field of action."

An highway shall be there, and a way, and it shall be called The way of holiness; the unclean shall not pass over it; but it shall be for those. —Isaiah 35:8

GOD SHED HIS GRACE ON THEE

Robert Frost, in his poetry, captured the essence of America just as Norman Rockwell did in his illustrations. In 1961, President-elect John Kennedy picked the eighty-seven-year-old Frost to read some of his verses at Kennedy's inauguration.

Frost believed that we in America have been blessed by God, and because of it, Americans have a special obligation to live up to our mission.

On that snowy January morning in Washington, D.C., Robert Frost recited these words: "The land was ours before we were the land's."

Where wast thou when I laid the foundations of the earth? Declare, if thou hast understanding. —Job 38:4

THE IRON LADY

In 1979 Margaret Thatcher became the first female prime minister of Great Britain. Three years later the Argentine government attacked the Falkland Islands, endangering the lives of British subjects. Against the advice of her foreign secretary and cabinet, Thatcher decided to defend the Falklands, and under her leadership Britain prevailed.

In 1983 she proposed that public-housing rental units be allowed to become the private property of their tenants. City councils were adamantly opposed. The consensus in her own cabinet was that the tenants, unlike the city government, would allow the units to erode into disrepair and become slums.

Thatcher believed that consensus is often a synonym for cowardice. She did what she thought was right, and it forever changed the political landscape of England.

You shall not follow a majority in wrongdoing.
                                            —Exodus 23:2 NRSV

A President's Plea

It was March 1933, the occasion of Governor Franklin Roosevelt's inauguration as the 32nd president. The country was gripped in the despair of the Depression. Huge crowds waited in the capital; and across the nation, millions gathered around their radio sets.

Governor Roosevelt had asked his "brain truster," Raymond Moley, to draft remarks. His old aide and friend, Judge Sam Rosenman, did not like the draft and wrote a different one for the Inaugural Address.

Neither draft had the lines that would come to epitomize the hope offered by the new president. Roosevelt wrote those opening lines himself: "Let me assert my firm belief that the only thing we have to fear is fear itself."

Fear not, and be not dismayed at this great multitude; for the battle is not yours but God's.—2 Chronicles 20:15 RSV

THE FATHER FORGIVES

Miguel Pro was a priest who braved the Mexican government's persecution of Catholics in the 1920s. Authorities vainly tried to arrest him, but he was a man of many disguises—blue-collar mechanic, elderly aristocratic gentleman, and even policeman. Sometimes, as a policeman, he would bring sacraments to prisoners. Once when a police car was chasing him while he was in a taxi, he told the driver to stop. Father Miguel rolled out, lit a cigar, and, taking the arm of a surprised young lady, began strolling down the avenue. The police car drove on.

In November 1927, the government finally captured him. Without a trial, he was condemned to death on trumped-up charges. At his execution, a policeman asked Father Miguel for his forgiveness, which Pro freely gave.

Just before the hail of bullets from the firing squad, he was heard to shout, "May God forgive my enemies. Long live Christ!"

The genuineness of your faith—being more precious than gold that, though perishable, is tested by fire—may be found to result in praise and glory and honor when Jesus Christ is revealed.

—1 Peter 1:7 NRSV

On Second Thought

Some of us have heard of the words spoken by the head of the U.S. Patent Office, Charles Duell, in 1899: "Everything that could be invented has been invented."

What about some other infamous predictions?

Gary Cooper said, "*Gone with the Wind* will be the biggest flop in Hollywood history."

Or, speaking of Hollywood, what about H. M. Warner, a head of Warner Brothers a decade earlier, who said in 1927, "Who wants to hear actors talk?"

Or in politics, former President Cleveland opined in 1905, "Sensible and responsible women do not want to vote."

Or in sports, Hall of Famer Tris Speaker said of Babe Ruth in 1921, "Babe Ruth made a big mistake when he gave up pitching."

Now faith is the substance of things hoped for, the evidence of things not seen. —Hebrews 11:1

A Red-blooded Hero

Some people may label the races of the world by color: white for Caucasian, black for African, yellow for Asian. But the blood of all is red! Oh yes, there may be types—O, A, B, and AB—but these transcend racial lines.

And in God's design, blood contains platelets active in the clotting process. We owe this knowledge to an African American scientist, Dr. Charles Drew, who discovered the process in 1940. Partly because of that discovery, blood banks were set up in hospitals and have saved countless lives.

In 1942 Drew spoke out against the American Red Cross, which had announced that it would exclude African Americans as donors to its national blood program. Because of Drew and others, the Red Cross reversed its policy.

It has been said that Drew, the "father of the blood bank," died when he was refused blood after an auto accident in Greensboro, North Carolina, in 1950. That is not true: he died before blood could have been administered. But it is true that Maltheus Avery, a 24-year-old student in Greensboro, died eight months later after another auto accident. Blood was not given to Avery because of his color.

So the question remains: Would Drew have received the same treatment?

And he made him a coat of many colours. —Genesis 37:3

IF AT FIRST YOU DON'T SUCCEED

In 1896, twelve-year-old Harry Truman was a piano student in Independence, Missouri. His teacher took him to see the world-celebrated pianist, Ignace Paderewski, who was performing in Kansas City. Afterward, the teacher took Truman to meet Paderewski. The Polish concert pianist asked Truman to play a piece. Truman played it. Paderewski shook his head. He played it again. Paderewski said, "No." The third time Truman played, Paderewski clapped his hands.

Four decades later, President Roosevelt sent his vice president to meet Paderewski. At that time, the former prime minister of Poland had just escaped his conquered country and arrived in New York.

"It is an honor to meet the vice president of the United States," said Paderewski.

"No," said Truman, "you met me before. I was the boy that you had play a piece three times before you were satisfied."

Seest thou a man diligent in his business? He shall stand before kings. —Proverbs 22:29

OLD MASTER

Anna Mary Robertson had led a hard life. She left home at the age of twelve and went to work as a cook and maid for other families. At seventeen, she married a harsh man, Thomas Moses, on a New York farm.

The newly married couple found work on a North Carolina farm. They were caretakers. When her husband died, she, in her late fifties, took over the farm. Her canned fruit won prizes at the local fair and so did her embroidery. But at age seventy-eight, her arthritis was so advanced that she had to quit.

But the widow Moses was not the type to sit in a rocking chair. She picked up a paintbrush and tried to put on canvas her experiences. And so it was that Grandma Moses found her legacy.

When I am old and greyheaded, O God, forsake me not.
—Psalm 71:18

V FOR VALOR

In August 1964, General Eisenhower paid a visit to Winston Churchill in the hospital. Churchill, in his ninetieth year, had suffered a stroke following his resignation from Parliament in July. The seizure had taken his voice.

When General Eisenhower entered Churchill's hospital suite, his old friend's eyes lit up in recognition. Sir Winston said nothing, but put his right hand on the bedside table next to him. Eisenhower could see that Churchill was a dying man: his sagging body was propped up against the back of the bed, and his face was flaccid with nine decades of infirmities.

On the bedside table, Churchill's small pink hand reached out for Eisenhower's. No words were uttered—the two men silently relived the battles they fought together for the ideals they mutually cherished. No words could have been more eloquent and poignant than the mute handclasp between two nations, two leaders, and two friends.

After nine minutes, Churchill unclasped his hand and slowly waved it in a "V" sign. Eisenhower went to the door. He said to the British aide who had accompanied him, "I just said goodbye to Winston, but you never say farewell to courage."

The wicked flee when no man pursueth: but the righteous are bold as a lion. —Proverbs 28:1

THE PREACHER INSPIRES A PRESIDENT

In the spring of 1854 in Boston, the distinguished abolitionist preacher Theodore Parker delivered a sermon in Faneuil Hall. In it he said, "Democracy is a government of all the people, by all the people, for all the people."

Parker adapted the phrase from the works of John Wycliffe, who rendered one of the first translations in English of the Bible. In the introduction Wycliffe wrote, "The Bible is of all the people, by all the people, for all the people."

The words by Wycliffe shaped Parker's definition of democracy that day in Boston. In the audience was a lawyer visiting from Illinois. Billy Herndon jotted down the sentence and gave this to his Springfield law partner, Abraham Lincoln.

Nine years later at a memorial battlefield in Gettysburg, Lincoln would use those same words: "Government of the people, by the people, and for the people shall not perish from the earth."

Where there is no vision, the people perish. —Proverbs 29:18

A Woman Named George

Mary Evans wanted all her life to write. Her strict evangelist father lectured her that writing was not women's work and was against the will of God.

Evans married to break away from her father's intolerance. Still, most publishers would not accept manuscripts from a woman. So she submitted hers under a man's name, George Eliot. Her first great novel, published in 1859, was *Adam Bede,* followed by *The Mill on the Floss* and *Silas Marner,* which established her, along with Charles Dickens, as one of the preeminent Victorian novelists.

One of George Eliot's characters expressed her resolve: "Any coward can fight a battle when he's sure of winning, but give me a man who has pluck to fight when he's sure of losing."

Of making many books there is no end; and much study is a weariness of the flesh. —Ecclesiastes 12:12

OLD BUT BOLD

Retirement? I would rather call it "commencement." At high schools and colleges, when you graduate, it's commencement—a beginning of a new chapter, a new challenge.

Retirement at age sixty-five? If it had been required in England in 1940, Churchill would not have been prime minister. He was sixty-seven—and without him, Britain would not have survived. That "old man" Churchill gave Britain its finest hour.

What about Picasso? He was still painting at ninety. George Bernard Shaw was still writing plays to be staged in New York and London at ninety-one. The Athenian dramatist Sophocles wrote a play at ninety.

As Churchill said, "To resign is not to retire."

You shall rise up before the hoary head, and honor the face of an old man, and you shall fear your God. —Leviticus 19:32 RSV

HE STOOPS TO CONQUER

Some weeks after President Ronald Reagan was shot in 1981, Vice President George Bush called on him at George Washington University Hospital in Washington, D.C.

Bush was astonished to find the President of the United States on his knees, mopping up the floor. He asked, "What are you doing, Mr. President?"

"Well, George," replied Reagan, "I've been getting only sponge baths, and I felt so dirty that I crawled into the tub. Some of the dirty water slopped over onto the floor, and I didn't want some nurse getting the dickens for it."

Better it is to be of an humble spirit with the lowly, than to divide the spoil with the proud. —Proverbs 16:19

A Friend in High Places

During the Civil War, President Abraham Lincoln received hundreds of appeals for pardons from soldiers who were sentenced to death by a military tribunal. The appeals were invariably supported by letters from congressmen, ministers, and town leaders. One day, a single sheet came before him—an appeal by a nineteen-year-old soldier without any supporting documents.

"What?" exclaimed the president. "Has this man no friend?"

"No, sir, not one," said the adjutant.

"Then," said Lincoln, signing the document, "I will be his friend."

Blessed are the merciful, for they will receive mercy. —Matthew 5:7 NRSV

A WARRIOR'S WISDOM

In the early 1800s the most famous Native American warrior was Tecumseh, chief of the Shawnee nation.

Agents of the federal government entreated Chief Tecumseh to sell the lands upon which his people dwelled and gained their sustenance.

"Sell a country!" exclaimed Tecumseh. "Why not sell the air, the clouds, the great sea?"

He chose to fight instead. The overwhelming might of the Americans defeated him, and the victor, General William Henry Harrison, was nicknamed "Tippecanoe" after the battle that defeated Tecumseh. In 1840 Harrison and his running mate, John Tyler, would win the White House on the alliterative slogan "Tippecanoe and Tyler too."

Harrison would only last a month as president, dying a few weeks after his inaugural address. His words are not remembered, but the words of the chief he defeated still have resonance today.

God saw everything that he had made, and indeed, it was very good. —Genesis 1:31 NRSV

THE SUNRISE CHAIR

At the close of the Constitutional Convention, the oldest delegate, Benjamin Franklin, slowly made his way to the front of the State House, now known as Independence Hall.

The eighty-year-old "grandfather of our country," as he had been called, pointed to the chair at the head table where General Washington, the presiding officer, had usually sat. The chair featured on its back the design of a sun low on the horizon with the rays extending out.

"Gentlemen," he said, "during the last few months, I have often wondered whether the picture was that of a rising or setting sun. But now at length I have the happiness to know," concluded Franklin, "it is a rising and not a setting sun."

I will give them one heart, and I will put a new spirit within you; and I will take the stony heart out of their flesh, and will give them an heart of flesh: That they may walk in my statutes, and keep mine ordinances, and do them: and they shall be my people, and I will be their God. —Ezekiel 11:19-20

THE JOLLY QUEEN MUM

The most popular member of the British royal family in recent years was not Queen Elizabeth II. No, it was not even the late Princess Di. It was the mother of the Queen, or, as she was referred to by the British public, "the Queen Mum." This petite figure with the huge hat won the hearts of her people with her infectious and jolly personality.

One incident was especially memorable. In World War II, during the Nazis' nightly bombing of London, government officials urged the Queen Mother (then Queen Elizabeth) and her husband, King George VI, to leave Buckingham Palace for Scotland or even Canada. The royal couple was adamant in their refusal. When asked later if the bombing had frightened her, Queen Elizabeth said no, she was glad, because now she was able to look East Londoners in the face.

In the spring of 2002, as Great Britain planned the Jubilee celebration of her daughter's fifty-year reign, the Queen Mother's health was failing. She told an old friend that she didn't want her death to dim the Jubilee. The ailing queen slipped away on Easter Sunday, a good two and a half months before the Jubilee.

The Queen Mother died as she lived, with a smile on her face. She was never one to ruin a party.

A merry heart doeth good like a medicine: but a broken spirit drieth the bones. —Proverbs 17:22

EYE TO EYE WITH TRUTH

As a young politician, Lee Atwater had two ambitions: to elect a president of the United States and to be National Chairman of his party before he was forty. He did both when he chaired George H. W. Bush's winning presidential campaign in 1988 and a year later was the G.O.P. National Chairman. Shortly thereafter, he developed a malignant brain tumor.

Before he died, Lee Atwater wrote, "You can acquire all you want and still feel empty. What power wouldn't I trade for a little more time with my family? What price wouldn't I pay for an evening with friends? It took a deadly illness to put me eye to eye with that truth, but it is a truth that the country . . . can learn on my dime."

How can you believe when you accept glory from one another and do not seek the glory that comes from the one who alone is God? —John 5:44 NRSV

THE MINISTER MARTYR

There is a handsome, imposing church in an African American neighborhood of west Philadelphia called St. Cyprian. Now, we see all the time churches named St. Matthew's, St. Mark's, and St. John's. But St. Cyprian? Well, he was the first African saint.

In 249 Cyprian, a famous orator, was elected Bishop of Carthage, the largest church in Africa. But the next year Decius, the new emperor, imposed the persecution of Christians, beginning with the execution of Fabian, the Bishop of Rome. The persecution spread to Africa with the edict that everyone give sacrifice to the Roman gods. Cyprian led his flock in resistance. For it he was tried by the Proconsul and beheaded in 258, the first African bishop to be crowned by martyrdom.

Whosoever shall deny me before men, him will I also deny before my Father which is in heaven. —Matthew 10:33

THE COMPASS OF COLUMBUS

"It is hard to imagine in this century the courage it took in the fifteenth century to sail west in unexplored, uncharted waters in the fragile vessels." These were the words of Astronaut Michael Collins, who traveled to the moon in 1969.

Columbus wrote that he was sustained by more than his maps and mathematics. It was his faith, and he was rewarded by that faith.

He wrote of his discovery when he returned, "He made me His Messenger of the new Heaven and Earth, and revealed those places to me."

Also I heard the voice of the Lord, saying, Whom shall I send, and who will go for us? Then said I, Here am I; send me.—Isaiah 6:8

FILL IN THE BLANKS

There is a famous painting of the signing of the Declaration of Independence that hangs in the White House outside the Oval Office. The painting is unusual because the artist died before he could complete it. Many of the figures in the background of the scene are only sketched in or left blank.

President Eisenhower had the painting hung because it reminds us of a profound truth. The American Dream is unfinished business, with important roles still open for each of us to play. In Eisenhower's mind, all of us are in that picture. It was not just the Founding Fathers who pledged to bring fulfillment to the promise of that document. All of us must sign on to make the American dream a reality.

Proclaim liberty throughout all the land unto all the inhabitants thereof. —Leviticus 25:10

NURTURING

THE TEACHER AND THE TAILOR

Eliza McCardle was a schoolteacher in Greeneville, Tennessee, who believed that her greatest role was shaping and directing the purpose of her students. But her most famous pupil was not a student; it was the nearly illiterate tailor she married. She saw in him, when few else did, the potential and promise of a future leader. His name was Andrew Johnson.

With her nurturing and coaching, Johnson rose from municipal office to become governor of Tennessee. As a pro-Union Democratic Party governor in a state that was divided in its loyalties, he would be picked by President Abraham Lincoln to be Lincoln's running mate on the newly named Union ticket in 1864.

As vice president, Andrew Johnson was one of the national leaders, along with President Lincoln and Secretary of State William Seward, targeted by John Wilkes Booth for assassination in 1865. Johnson survived to put into effect Lincoln's Reconstruction policies, which included political freedom for former slaves.

Johnson was later impeached and acquitted by one vote. Finishing his term as president, he owed his rise to national office to his resolute support of Lincoln's policies and, always, to his wife and teacher, Eliza McCardle.

He who finds a wife finds a good thing,
and obtains favor from the LORD. —Proverbs 18:22 NRSV

REAGAN'S FAVORITE FILM LINE

Ronald Reagan never won an Academy Award for his acting, although some think his performance in the 1942 movie *Kings Row* merited one.

It was the story of a young man who had his legs amputated. The young man did not despair, however. Reagan's favorite line in the film is not one that he uttered, but he would quote it the rest of his life.

In the movie, the character played by Reagan seeks advice from an older man who has taken an interest in him. The man says, "Some people grow up, and some grow older."

And Reagan would say, "I believe that God intends us all to grow up, and there are times when all of us ought to take stock and see if we are growing up or merely growing older."

The hoary head is a crown of glory, if it be found in the way of righteousness. —Proverbs 16:31

GENTLEMAN GENERAL

During the Civil War, Robert E. Lee was riding on a train to Richmond to see Jefferson Davis. He was seated in the rear of the car, and all the other places were filled with officers and soldiers. An old woman, humbly dressed, boarded the coach at a rural station. No seat was offered her, and so she stood in the back of the car. Immediately, Lee stood up and offered her his seat. One after another of the men in the car offered the general his seat.

"No, gentlemen," he replied. "If there is none for this lady, there can be none for me."

All of you, have unity of spirit, sympathy, love for one another, a tender heart, and a humble mind. —1 Peter 3:8 NRSV

TEDDY BALLGAME

One of the greatest hitters in the history of baseball was Ted Williams, the last batter to hit over .400. He was born in San Diego, and his Mexican mother named him after Theodore Roosevelt. Like Roosevelt, he was a war hero. Six of his most productive years were spent as a Marine pilot in World War II and Korea. Yet, despite that, he racked up many Hall of Fame records.

The Boston Red Sox star fittingly played his last game in Fenway Park, on September 28, 1960. He had refused "Farewell to Ted" days in his last games around the American League. But he yielded to pregame ceremonies in Boston because the proceeds would be given to the Jimmy Fund, an organization he founded that supported handicapped children.

On his last appearance at the plate in the ninth inning, Ted hit a home run off Jack Fisher of the Orioles. Ted rounded the bases, making no acknowledgment to the fans, who pleaded for him to come out of the dugout to wave a farewell. Even the umpire directed Ted to make an appearance. But Ted refused. He remembered his mother's telling him what Theodore Roosevelt once said, "Speak softly and carry a big stick."

The man who referred to himself as "Teddy Ballgame" let his stick do the talking.

As the body without the spirit is dead, so faith without works is dead also. —James 2:26

But for Eleanor

But for his wife, Eleanor, Franklin Delano Roosevelt would never have become president.

In 1920, as assistant secretary of the Navy, Roosevelt was chosen to be the Democratic vice presidential candidate with Governor James Cox of Ohio. Though the Cox-Roosevelt ticket was defeated, Roosevelt was established as the most popular new personality in the Democratic Party.

Six months after the election, however, Roosevelt was stricken by polio. His legs were paralyzed, and his strength severely diminished. Roosevelt's mother and friends urged him to retire from political life. But Eleanor Roosevelt was adamantly opposed.

In 1924, at her urging, he gave the nominating speech for Governor Al Smith. Smith lost the nomination that year but was successfully nominated in 1928. Smith then urged Roosevelt to run for governor of New York. Again Roosevelt's mother and friends urged him not to run. At Eleanor's insistence, Roosevelt ran anyway, and his victory paved the way for his election as president in 1932.

Said Eleanor Roosevelt later, "No one can make you feel inferior without your consent."

Favour is deceitful, and beauty is vain: but a woman that feareth the LORD, she shall be praised. . . . Let her own works praise her in the gates. —Proverbs 31:30-31

THE ACORN AND A COLLEGE

In the sixteenth century, Queen Elizabeth noted the presence of Sir Walter Mildmay, who had been missing from court for some time.

Mildmay, who had been away establishing Emmanuel College at Cambridge, replied, "Madam, I have been away planting an acorn, and when it becomes an oak, God only knows what will be the fruit of it."

In the morning sow thy seed, and in the evening withhold not thine hand. —Ecclesiastes 11:6

THE SIMPLE TRUTH

The eminent religious philosopher Karl Barth was invited to address a gathering of clergymen and lay leaders of various Protestant faiths.

Afterward, a journalist in attendance asked the erudite theologian if he could express in one sentence the fruit of his many years of academic studies.

Barth replied that all the knowledge he had gathered was a repeat of what he learned in an old Sunday school hymn as a child. "Jesus loves me, this I know, 'cause the Bible tells me so."

This is a faithful saying, and worthy of all acceptation, that Christ Jesus came into the world to save sinners.

—1 Timothy 1:15

MIGHTY MOLLY

The name of Mary Ludwig Hays, who became the wife of John Hays, is forgotten in history. But her nickname of Molly Pitcher is still remembered. Molly Pitcher is honored because she carried pitchers of water to help the revolutionary soldiers defeat the English on June 28, 1778, at the Battle of Monmouth in New Jersey.

She had come to the battlefield to give food and sustenance to her husband, John, who was manning a cannon. She found him in the middle of a smoke-covered battlefield, prostrate from heatstroke, and unconscious. Putting on her husband's cap to hide her hair, she donned his jacket and took over his cannon post for the rest of the day until the battle was won.

Yea, though I walk through the valley of the shadow of death, I will fear no evil: for thou art with me; thy rod and thy staff they comfort me. —Psalm 23:4

THE BIBLE BOOTLEGGER

He was known as Brother Andrew. The Dutch evangelist had dropped his last name during his Bible-smuggling days in Iron Curtain countries. He had found in those Soviet satellite countries that often even pastors of congregations lacked Bibles. So he organized a mass operation with other evangelical volunteers. The organization, now operating in forty-five countries, has distributed over a million Bibles.

Once, as a border guard searched his car in Poland in 1955, Brother Andrew prayed, "Lord, you have made blind eyes see— now I ask you to make seeing eyes blind." The guard, apparently seeing nothing to arouse his suspicions, waved Brother Andrew through.

All scripture is given by inspiration of God, and is profitable for doctrine, for reproof, for correction, for instruction in righteousness.
—2 Timothy 3:16

THE MEXICAN LINCOLN

In Washington, D.C., amid the statues of presidents, generals, and other American heroes, there is among them a foreign leader who is honored. He is Benito Juarez, whose monument is near our State Department.

Juarez is sometimes called "the Abraham Lincoln of Mexico," but his public career to lift the lives of the poor and oppressed began before Lincoln's. Juarez was the first democratically elected president of Mexico. Did he possess the charismatic qualities of good looks and oratory to achieve high office? No, unless you consider character, integrity, and fortitude charismatic.

Actually, he was short—four feet, ten inches—and ugly. His enemies said he looked like a toad. And because of his poor Spanish, which carried a heavy Indian accent, he had once been limited to menial jobs. This Zapotec Indian, born in a poor mountain region, went on to educate himself as a lawyer and dared to run for office in 1833 for the provincial legislature in the state of Oaxaca.

There he opposed a bill offered by a follower of the dictator Santa Anna. He concluded, saying, "Libertad, humanidad, dignidad (liberty, humanity, dignity)!" The next day he was arrested for conspiring to incite the Indians to revolt. Later he was released and continued to fight for Indian rights. He went on to serve as president of Mexico for two terms.

The stone which the builders refused is become the head stone of the corner. —Psalm 118:22

BEAUTY IN THE EYE OF THE BEHOLDER

In the spring of 1863, a delegation from the Union League Club of Philadelphia called on President Lincoln. The organization was established by influential Philadelphians to support the policies of Lincoln. They had commissioned an artist named Edward Dalton Marchant to paint a portrait of the president.

Marchant had been staying at the White House for months while he worked on the portrait. During that time Marchant had come to idolize the embattled chief executive, who was endeavoring to bring to fruition the promise of the Emancipation Proclamation he had signed months earlier. Now that the painting was completed, three members of the Union League came to inspect the work of Marchant.

The painting imparted a measure of nobility to Lincoln's homely features. Lincoln looked at it and said to the artist in the presence of the Union League visitors, "I presume in the painting of your beautiful portrait, you took your idea of me from my principles and not from my person."

The LORD seeth not as man seeth; for man looketh on the outward appearance, but the LORD looketh on the heart. —1 Samuel 16:7

THE CARPENTER'S DAUGHTER

In 1969 Golda Meir would become the first female prime minister of Israel. She was the leader in 1973 when Israel triumphed over the invading Egyptian and Syrian armies.

After her election, Meir was invited by Pope Paul VI to make an unprecedented visit to the Vatican. During the visit she said to the Pope, "Think of this! The daughter of a Milwaukee carpenter meeting His Holiness the Pope."

The Pope replied, "Prime Minister, in the Vatican, carpentry is considered the noblest of trades."

I Deborah arose, that I arose a mother in Israel. —Judges 5:7

THE STILL, SMALL VOICE

In 1964, the last year of his life, the eighty-four-year-old General Douglas MacArthur was greeted by reporters on his birthday. They asked him what he saw to be the central issue facing humanity.

The general replied, "The world is in constant conspiracy against the brave. It's the age-old struggle—the roar of the crowd on one side, and the voice of your conscience on the other."

Know ye not that the friendship of the world is enmity with God? Whosoever therefore will be a friend of the world is the enemy of God. —James 4:4

THE BIG LITTLE WOMAN

At a White House reception in 1863 President Abraham Lincoln noted a woman less than five feet tall standing next to a man in a clergy collar. He immediately knew it was Harriet Beecher Stowe and her husband, the Reverend Calvin Stowe. Four years before, Harriet Beecher Stowe had published her novel *Uncle Tom's Cabin.*

"Are you the little woman," asked the president with a chuckle, "who is the cause of this big war?"

More than her husband or the other abolitionist preachers, Harriet Beecher Stowe did the most to inflame American opinion against the wretched institution of slavery.

Righteousness exalteth a nation. —Proverbs 14:34

UNARMED BUT UNAFRAID

In August 1945, after the second atomic bomb, Emperor Hirohito surrendered on behalf of the Japanese people. President Harry Truman dispatched General Douglas MacArthur to Japan.

The general arrived at Narita Airport with a few of his staff. He commandeered an open limousine to take him on the forty-mile journey to Tokyo.

A half million Japanese soldiers were still armed. MacArthur's aides pressed him to take a bulletproof, closed car filled with machine guns or at least pistols to make the trip. MacArthur dismissed the warnings. He rode standing up past the hundreds of thousands of Japanese soldiers lining the highway to Tokyo. It was, Winston Churchill said later, a supreme display of courage.

Be strong and of a good courage. . . . And the LORD, he it is that doth go before thee; he will be with thee, he will not fail thee, neither forsake thee. —Deuteronomy 31:7-8

Presence of God

Right across from the White House, next to Lafayette Park, stands St. John's Episcopal Church. It was the church President Franklin D. Roosevelt attended.

Early one Sunday morning, the phone to the church rang. Rector John Magee answered it. A voice asked, "Will the president be in attendance?"

"No," answered Magee, "but God will. That is reason enough for attending."

Not forsaking the assembling of ourselves together, as the manner of some is; but exhorting one another. —Hebrews 10:25

Word of God

William Tyndale was a tutor in an English household. When an argument about Henry VIII's divorce arose, a visiting abbot challenged Tyndale, saying he had picked up some reform ideas at Oxford.

Tyndale replied that what was important was not what he thought but what the Bible says. The Abbot said no, that it was the pope's opinion that mattered. Tyndale answered that he heeded the Scripture, not the pope.

Whereupon Tyndale allegedly said something like, "If God spares my life, I will help the boy behind the plow know more of the scripture than you do."

So Tyndale left the household to work on a translation of the Bible into English from the original language. This was to be the first English Bible printed on a printing press.

Faith cometh by hearing, and hearing by the word of God.
—Romans 10:17

CONFUCIUS SAYS

Twenty-five hundred years ago, a new emperor assumed the throne of the Middle Kingdom. The young Chinese monarch called to his court his foremost advisor.

"O sage counselor, you have offered wisdom to my father and my grandfather. Today is my first day on the throne, what is the best advice you can give me?"

And Confucius replied, "Imperial Majesty, in difficult situations, you must first define the problem."

The words of wise men are heard in quiet more than the cry of him that ruleth among fools. —Ecclesiastes 9:17

WOOMY

A British youth was packed off to boarding school. A little while later, his nanny, Mrs. Everest, whom he called "Woomy" (for "woman"), was dismissed by his parents, even though there was a younger brother for whom she might have cared.

Although the youth was the grandson of a duke, he was given an allowance of only ten shillings a week while at boarding school. A couple of years later, he had saved enough from his allowance to send the ailing Mrs. Everest a ticket to London and a night's lodging.

As they walked on the quadrangle of Harrow School, the fifteen-year-old boy clasped Mrs. Everest's hand. She discouraged him from doing so, thinking that the other boys would make fun of him.

But Winston Churchill showed his courage at an early age. Resisting peer pressure, he continued clasping her hand, then kissed her and said he loved her. She lived only a few months longer. The picture of Woomy would stand on Churchill's bedside table the rest of his life.

Train up a child in the way he should go: and when he is old, he will not depart from it.—Proverbs 22:6

THE MASTER OF ESCAPE

Erich Weiss became known as the great Houdini, the master of escape. If he was locked into any jail, he could free himself in a matter of minutes.

One time, however, he failed. When the metal doors slammed shut behind him, he pulled from his belt a hidden piece of strong but flexible metal. But for thirty minutes, after trying all his tricks, he could not open the lock.

After three hours, he collapsed against the door. To his astonishment, it swung open. It had not been locked in the first place.

Ask, and it shall be given you; seek, and ye shall find; knock, and it shall be opened unto you.—Matthew 7:7

69

Second Fiddle

Leonard Bernstein, who was perhaps America's greatest conductor, once was asked what was the most difficult instrument in the orchestra to play. Bernstein thought for a moment and said, "Second fiddle. I can find many who want to play first violin, but few ask to be second. But without the second fiddle, there is no harmony."

The meek shall inherit the earth; and shall delight themselves in the abundance of peace. —Psalm 37:11

APRIL SHOWERS, MAY FLOWERS

At age forty in 1938, the Puerto Rican-born Luis Muñoz Marin was the most famous Spanish-writing journalist in New York. He was also a published poet. He was convinced by his friends in Puerto Rico to return to organize the political fight to give Puerto Ricans more voting rights, and to free the island from a semicolonial status to an associated-state relationship with the United States.

With the slogan "Bread, Land, and Liberty," Marin's party eventually won, and in 1948 he became the first popularly elected governor of Puerto Rico.

In 1950, when anarchists opposing Muñoz Marin broke into the House of Representatives in Washington, killing one congressman and others, Governor Muñoz Marin said to the doomsayers in Puerto Rico, "Tell the umbrella-mongers: When has an umbrella ever kept the rains from entering a heart and shaping it with dreams?"

I have multiplied visions, and used similitudes, by the ministry of the prophets.—Hosea 12:10

No Time Like the Present

In 1628, Captain John Smith, the pioneer of Virginia, wrote in his diary while sailing up the Chesapeake Bay, "I would rather be a settler in America than a Good Queen Bess on the throne of England. Here one can spread his wings and soar like an eagle. These are the times for men to live."

This is the beginning of a new millennium, and these are great times for men and women to live.

For, behold, I create new heavens and a new earth.

—Isaiah 65:17

Faith and Fight

Todd Beamer, a committed Christian, was one of those brave passengers on September 11, 2001, on United Airlines Flight 93 who resisted the hijacking terrorists. He made cellular calls to his wife, alerting authorities to the dead pilot and copilot. When he learned of the attack on the World Trade Center, he and others decided to jump the hijackers. Beamer said, "I don't think we are going to get out of this thing. I'm going to have to go out on faith." Then he said, "Let's roll."

Later his widow, Lisa, going through his things, found in Todd's desk this quotation from Teddy Roosevelt:

> The credit belongs to the man who is actually in the arena, who strives valiantly, who knows the great enthusiasms, the great devotions, and spends himself in a worthy cause; . . . who, at worst, if he fails, at least fails while daring greatly, so that his place shall never be with those cold and timid souls who know neither victory nor defeat.

Be strong and of a good courage, fear not, nor be afraid of them: for the LORD thy God, he it is that doth go with thee; he will not fail thee, nor forsake thee.—Deuteronomy 31:6

Just a Girl

In 1428 a sixteen-year-old girl from Orleans, France, said she had been visited in her dreams by saints and angels, who said she would lead an army driving the English from France. The Bishop laughed at her, saying she was just a girl.

But the girl persisted. She recruited an army and did indeed force the English to leave. Later she led an army of 12,000 to Rheims, enabling Charles VII to be crowned king. A short time later she was captured, tried for heresy, and burned at the stake.

But her name went down in history: Jeanne d'Arc, or Joan of Arc.

The LORD is on my side; I will not fear: what can man do unto me? —Psalm 118:6

BACKSIDE IKE

In March 1944, General Dwight D. Eisenhower was scheduled to make an appearance before troops in Norfolk, England. It was raining that morning. As Eisenhower made his way to the little platform from which he was to deliver a few remarks, he slipped in the mud and fell. The troops tried to stifle their reaction. As Ike got back on his feet, he wiped the mud off his seat. When he finished, he let loose a big guffaw.

That triggered gales of laughter from the soldiers. Ike then gave his famous two-armed wave and pushed his way into the troops, shaking hands. There were no remarks delivered. It was, as Ike later said, "the best morale-lifting appearance I ever made."

A time to weep, and a time to laugh.—Ecclesiastes 3:4

THE DAY OF JUDGMENT

In Hartford, Connecticut, one day in 1780, the skies at noon turned from blue to gray. By mid-afternoon, the city had darkened over so densely that, in that religious age, people fell on their knees and begged a final blessing before the end of the world descended.

The Connecticut House of Delegates was in session. There was pandemonium, and many of the Connecticut House were calling for adjournment. The Speaker of the House, Colonel Caleb Davenport, rose to his feet and silenced the din with these words:

"The Day of Judgment is either at hand or it is not at hand. If it is not, there is no need for adjournment. If it is, I choose to be found by my God doing my duty. I entertain the motion, therefore, that candles be brought to enlighten this hall of democracy."

Your word is a lamp to my feet and a light to my path.
—Psalm 119:105 NRSV

THE MAJOR AND THE CORPORAL

In October 1916, in a World War I trench in Belgium, a British major paced, inspecting the condition of his regiment. Thirty yards away, a grubby German corporal twitched his mustache, waiting for orders.

One was Winston Churchill, the other Adolph Hitler. One would come to represent heroic magnitude in combating evil, the other evil itself. Two decades later they would meet again in World War II.

The face of the LORD is against evildoers,
to cut off the remembrance of them from the earth.
—Psalm 34:16 NRSV

FDR's "Conscience"

Unlike many First Ladies, Eleanor Roosevelt was an active participant in political life. She served as the president's arms and legs, traveling the county to inspect mines and assembly lines that her husband couldn't reach. She was also, FDR admitted, "my conscience," reminding him about the plight of displaced Jews in Europe and civil rights for African Americans.

When her husband died, Eleanor Roosevelt's championing of the downtrodden did not cease. Neither did her endeavors for peace. She was for many years the United States representative to the United Nations.

Adlai Stevenson, two-time Democratic candidate for president and her successor at the United Nations, said of her: "She would rather have lit one candle than curse the darkness."

"I am the light of the world: he that followeth me shall not walk in darkness, but shall have the light of life."—John 8:12

Sharing the Wealth

Perhaps the richest man in the world at the end of the nineteenth century was Andrew Carnegie, the Scottish emigrant who founded U.S. Steel. To his office in Pittsburgh, Pennsylvania, came a supplicant, requesting that Carnegie share a bit of his wealth.

Andrew Carnegie nodded in contemplation of the request. He wrote a note on a piece of paper and then called in his male secretary. The secretary retreated. The multi-millionaire Carnegie and his visitor chatted for a few minutes. Then the secretary returned with a check, which Carnegie handed to the man.

The check was for 32 cents—Carnegie's holdings divided by the world's population.

Later in his life, Carnegie used his wealth to build libraries and establish foundations such as the Carnegie Endowment for International Peace.

A sound heart is the life of the flesh: but envy the rottenness of the bones. —Proverbs 14:30

LATIMER'S LIGHT

Hugh Latimer became the Bishop of Worcester under Henry VIII. When Prince Edward succeeded Henry, Latimer worked with Thomas Cranmer in writing the *Book of Common Prayer.* But upon the accession of Queen Mary Tudor, Latimer was sent to the Tower of London and condemned for heresy, along with Nicholas Ridley and Thomas Cranmer.

As his executioners lit the flame to burn him at the stake, Latimer turned to Ridley and said, "Be of good courage and play the man; for we shall this day light such a candle by God's grace in England as I trust shall never be put out."

Therefore, my beloved brethren, be ye steadfast, unmoveable, always abounding in the work of the Lord, forasmuch as ye know that your labour is not in vain in the Lord. —1 Corinthians 15:58

THE POPE AND THE PRISONERS

Shortly after his election in 1958, Pope John XXIII informed the Vatican that he wanted to visit an Italian prison. His staff objected, saying no pope had ever done so.

Pope John replied that if they could not come to see him, then he must go to see them.

Whoever loves a brother or sister lives in the light, and in such a person there is no cause for stumbling. —1 John 2:10 NRSV

THE GOSPEL ACCORDING TO ANOTHER MARK

On his desk in the Oval Office, President Harry Truman kept a sign. His mother had told him what fellow Missourian Mark Twain once said to a Young People's Fellowship at the Brooklyn Presbyterian Church toward the end of Twain's life.

The sign read, "Always do right. This will gratify some people and astonish the rest."

It is no coincidence that when Truman was sworn in as president, he had the family Bible open to the words of the prophet Micah.

And what does the LORD require of you
but to do justice, and to love kindness,
and to walk humbly with your God? —Micah 6:8 NRSV

Sunday School "Swing"

For anyone who loves jazz, one of the all-time favorites to come out of New Orleans, Louisiana, is "When the Saints Come Marching In." We still can hear in our mind's memory the raspy voice of Louis Armstrong belting out those lines. "Lord, how I want to be in the number, / when the saints go marching in."

You may be surprised to learn that the words did not originate in New Orleans but in a Sunday school in Williamsport, Pennsylvania. When a young girl failed to answer Sunday school attendance call in the Pine Street Methodist Church in 1881, a lay revivalist, James Black, was inspired to compose, "When the Roll Is Called Up Yonder."

The Salvation Army picked up the catchy Sunday school song, and it found its way to New Orleans, where those jazz trumpeters worked their magic.

Wherefore seeing we also are compassed about with so great a cloud of witnesses . . . let us run with patience the race that is set before us. —Hebrews 12:1

Last Words

In the North Carolina state museum in Raleigh, a letter that appears to be written in red ink is displayed under glass.

The letter is by an eighteen-year-old soldier. But the red is not ink; it's the blood from his wound in battle. The dying cavalryman in Chancellorsville used his sword to pen his last words.

"Tell my poppy that I died with me facing the enemy."

For we wrestle not against flesh and blood, but against principalities, against powers, against the rulers of the darkness of this world, against spiritual wickedness in high places. —Ephesians 6:12

THE WINGS OF VICTORY

In April 1945, Prime Minister Winston Churchill heard by telephone that his good friend and staunch partner, President Franklin Roosevelt, had died. Roosevelt's death came as the Nazi regime and its tyranny were crumbling.

With tears in his eyes, Churchill said to his wife, Clementine, "He died on the wings of victory, Clemmie, but he saw those wings and heard them flapping."

Death is swallowed up in victory. O death, where is thy sting? O grave, where is thy victory? —1 Corinthians 15:54-55

TRAVAIL AND TRIUMPH

The life of Abraham Lincoln was riddled with disappointment and defeat. In 1832, he ran for the Illinois state legislature; he lost. Two years later, he managed to win and then was reelected. But in 1837, the general store he ran went bankrupt.

In 1840, he won a seat in the U.S. Congress. But he didn't run for reelection, since his Springfield constituency heavily favored the Mexican War, which he opposed.

In 1855, he tried for the U.S. Senate; he lost. The next year, he bid to be nominated as vice president in the new Republican Party; he lost.

In 1859, he challenged Stephen Douglas for the U.S. Senate seat; he lost.

In 1860, he was elected President.

He that endureth to the end shall be saved. —Matthew 10:22

THE SNAKE AND THE FLOWER

Chinese is a language that uses more than 30,000 pictographs instead of letters. The "pictures" slowly evolved into stylized representations.

In Mandarin Chinese, the word for *crisis* is composed of two such stylized characters. The first is "wo," picturing a snake; the second is "jei," picturing the small bud of a flower.

Sometimes only in dangers or difficulties do we find new resources and opportunities.

Beloved, think it not strange concerning the fiery trial which is to try you, as though some strange thing happened unto you: But rejoice, inasmuch as ye are partakers of Christ's sufferings; that, when his glory shall be revealed, ye may be glad also with exceeding joy. —1 Peter 4:12-13

THE STRONG SILENT MAN

Like Moses, another man who led his people out of bondage, George Washington was not adept with words.

At twelve Washington was six feet, three inches, probably the tallest person in Virginia, but he was still a boy. Reared in a fatherless home with only a few years of schooling, he felt tongue-tied in the presence of his seniors, who had the smooth patter of country squires and plantation cavaliers.

For much of his life, nods, gestures, and monosyllabic replies were his modes of communication. He grew into the prototype of the strong silent man.

In 1786, General George Washington, who had led the Continental Army to win the War of Independence, was elected President of the Constitutional Convention. He was invited afterwards to give a speech. General Washington delivered a one-sentence speech: "Let us raise a standard to which the wise and honest can repair."

I am slow of speech and slow of tongue. —Exodus 4:10 NRSV

THE BRIGADIER AND THE BIBLE

In the First World War, one of the lesser-known general officers was Brigadier Clive Whittlesey. Yet no officer commanded
more devotion from his men.

During the war, the ramrod, white-haired brigadier was
thought to be a bit of a martinet in his enforcement of discipline.
One example of that, which his soldiers did not understand, was
his requirement that they memorize the Ninety-first Psalm.
Whittlesey, who was a regular reader of scripture, had copies of
the Ninety-first Psalm passed out on little cards. He frequently
called on the soldiers to recite it. If they failed, they were given
guard duty and later had to appear before him and deliver it from
memory.

The familiar psalm includes the following verses: "He shall
cover thee with his feathers, and under his wings shalt thou trust:
his truth shall be thy shield and buckler. Thou shalt not be afraid
for the terror by night; nor for the arrow that flieth by day; nor for
the pestilence that walketh in darkness. . . . A thousand shall fall
at thy side, and ten thousand by thy right hand; but it shall not
come nigh thee" (vv. 4-7).

It is an amazing thing that all the men of his regiment survived
the war—the only British regiment in the war to have no fatalities.

*The Lord gave the word: great was the company of those that
published it. —Psalm 68:11*

EARTH ANGEL

More American soldiers died either from battle or infectious wounds in the Civil War than from all other wars put together. The wounds of these soldiers required nursing and care. When Clara Barton, a Massachusetts schoolteacher in her forties, left her job and offered to help nurse the men, military and civil authorities initially turned her down, since women had not previously been allowed in hospitals. Victorian proprieties deemed the sight of a naked man unbefitting the frail sensibilities of any woman. However, the need was so great that the authorities ultimately relented. By 1864 Barton was named superintendent of Union Army nurses and became known as the "Angel of the Battlefield."

In 1869 Barton traveled to Europe, where she learned about a new organization called the Red Cross. Ultimately she went on to found the American Red Cross, and she served as its president for twenty-two years. The organization performed heroic duty, notably during the 1889 Johnstown flood, for many years the greatest natural disaster in American history. By that time in her sixties, Barton was told by doctors and urged by friends not to go to the western Pennsylvania city. She went anyway, and in so doing widened the role of the Red Cross to provide nursing relief and care, not only in war but also during natural disasters.

He healeth the broken in heart, and bindeth up their wounds.
—Psalm 147:3

ABE'S BEARD

We should listen to children. From their innocence often comes the truth, untempered by politeness or fear of hurting feelings.

During the campaign in 1860, Abraham Lincoln once received a letter from a little girl, Grace Bedell of Westfield, New York. She said that she had seen his portrait and thought he would look more distinguished with a beard.

Lincoln replied that he would consider it but not during the campaign because it would look like "a silly affectation."

After the election, the clean-shaven President-elect let his beard grow. On his train trip to Washington, D.C., the train stopped in Westfield. Lincoln asked if the little girl was in the crowd. She was, and she was brought up to Lincoln. He thanked her for her advice and kissed her.

Better is a poor and a wise child than an old and foolish king, who will no more be admonished. —Ecclesiastes 4:13

DR. BILLY AND THE BIBLE

Dr. Billy Graham is one of the greatest preachers of our time. The evangelical leader has been the friend and counselor of every president from Lyndon Johnson to George W. Bush. But even Graham had his crisis of faith.

In 1949, Graham was at a fundamentalist retreat in the mountains near Los Angeles. The thirty-one-year-old preacher was lectured by Chuck Templeton, a Princeton Seminary minister and theologian, that Graham was fifty years out of date and that people no longer accepted the Bible as being inspired.

Graham answered that he wasn't even sure he believed in God.

Graham was questioning certain passages in the Bible that he could not quite accept. He knew he could not lead revivals in that frame of mind.

In crisis, he took the Bible one night on a walk into some deep woods.

As he said later, "I had the Bible in my hands, and I opened it and said, 'Lord, I don't understand all of this Bible. But I accept it all by faith. I accept it.' And at that moment, I had a tremendous conviction and faith."

My brethren, count it all joy when ye fall into divers temptations . . . the trying of your faith worketh patience. But let patience have her perfect work, that ye may be perfect and entire, wanting nothing. —James 1:2-4

GOOD QUEEN BESS

In the sixteenth century they used to say that the smartest king in Europe wore a skirt. They were referring to Elizabeth I of England. Daughter of the beheaded Anne Boleyn, Elizabeth was abandoned by her father, Henry VIII. As a child she was kept in confinement, sometimes in the Tower of London prison. When her half-sister Queen Mary ("Bloody Mary") died, Elizabeth assumed the throne.

As head of the Church of England, she managed to keep the Puritans and high-church Anglicans in the fold. She also succeeded in preventing the Catholic King Philip of Spain, the most powerful country in the world, from grabbing England and adding it to his empire.

At age thirty-five, as Philip's Spanish Armada approached England, Elizabeth visited her troops in the field.

"I know I have but the body of a weak and feeble woman," she told them, "but I have the heart of a king, and of a king of England, too; and think foul scorn that Parma or Spain, or any prince of Europe, should dare to invade the borders of my realms."

If the trumpet give an uncertain sound, who shall prepare himself to the battle?—1 Corinthians 14:8

O THOU OF "LARGE" FAITH

When Christopher Columbus returned to Spain in 1493, he wrote that as he sailed he learned to forget all his earlier knowledge and experience and put his trust in God and the Holy Scripture. Columbus wrote:

Neither reason nor mathematics nor maps of the world were of any help that I should fulfill this enterprise of the Indies. If you have faith, you may be confident of victory.

We walk by faith, not by sight. —2 Corinthians 5:7 NRSV

Farragut and Faith

In Washington, D.C., Farragut Circle is a well-traveled junction. It is named after Admiral David Farragut of Civil War fame.

Once during that war, Admiral Farragut called Captain Samuel DuPont into his office to have Captain DuPont account for his failure to take his gunboats into Charleston Harbor. DuPont listed five reasons why he didn't make the raid.

Farragut replied that there was another reason. When DuPont asked what it was, Farragut said DuPont did not believe he could do it.

Whatever is born of God conquers the world. And this is the victory that conquers the world, our faith. —*1 John 5:4 NRSV*

FORGIVENESS

THE PRISONER TURNED PREACHER

Jacob DeShazer learned the news of Pearl Harbor while doing K.P. duty as a sergeant on a base in San Diego. Later, as a pilot, he would volunteer to fly with Jimmy Doolittle in the first bombing of Japan. The historic flight was described in the book *Thirty Seconds Over Tokyo* by Ted Lawson. When the B-25 DeShazer was flying ran out of fuel, the crew bailed out. DeShazer was captured and imprisoned.

During his brutal imprisonment, he found God. Later he would say, "I believe heaven came down in that prison cell." He responded to his cruel prison guards with words of kindness.

Released in 1945, DeShazer vowed to return to Japan as a missionary, which he did with his wife in 1948. There he worked with Mitsoo Fochi, who was the former commander of the surprise attack on Pearl Harbor.

"You have heard that it was said, 'You shall love your neighbor and hate your enemy.' But I say to you, 'Love your enemies and pray for those who persecute you, so that you may be children of your Father in heaven.'"—Matthew 5:43-45 NRSV

NO FAIR-WEATHER FRIEND

Harry Truman rose from the position of county municipal judge to U.S. senator to vice president and went on to become a great president. But he owed his rise to the backing of Tom Prendergast, a powerful political boss in Kansas City. Prendergast went to jail for tax evasion in 1945, when Truman was vice president, and died shortly afterward.

Truman's advisors urged him not to attend his old friend and backer's funeral in early 1945, saying that the dignity of the country's second highest office would be diminished if he went. But Vice President Truman attended anyway. Truman said, "He was always my friend, and I have always been his."

A friend loveth at all times, and a brother is born for adversity.
—Proverbs 17:17

Voyage of Valor

In 1942 President Franklin D. Roosevelt conferred on General Douglas MacArthur the Congressional Medal of Honor for his heroic escape in a P.T. boat from the Philippines to Brisbane, Australia. General MacArthur's father had also earned the coveted medal for his gallantry in the Civil War.

But with all due respect to the general, we mustn't overlook the valor of his wife, Jean, who traveled in the same P.T. vessel with Japanese destroyers chasing them from behind and Japanese Zero fighting planes strafing them from above—with their one-year-old son, Arthur, in her lap. Was her courage any less?

Entreat me not to leave thee, or to return from following after thee: for whither thou goest, I will go; . . . thy people shall be my people, and thy God my God. —Ruth 1:16

Ageless Adage

"The earth is degenerating these days. Venality and corruption abound. Children no longer mind their parents. It is evident that the end of civilization is nearing."

And so the words written in cuneiform on an Assyrian tablet over five thousand years ago read like today's newspaper.

Lord, thou hast been our dwelling place in all generations. . . . Thou turnest man to destruction; and sayest, "Return, ye children of men." For a thousand years in thy sight are but as yesterday when it is past, and as a watch in the night. —Psalm 90:1, 3-4

VALOR AND THE VICAR OF ROME

On June 10, 1979, the first Polish pope, John Paul II, returned to his native land. Shortly before his trip, Poland, under pressure from the Soviet Union, had disbanded Solidarity, the union movement, and imposed martial law, hoping to stifle the Roman Catholic Church and the dissent of the people. Soviet armies were poised at Poland's border to reinforce the Polish government.

Despite warnings of the Polish authorities, Pope John Paul II declared to hundreds of thousands in Krakow:

> We must be strong with the strength of faith. We must be strong with the strength of hope. We must be strong with the strength of love. When we are strong with the strength of God, we need not be afraid.

It is better to trust in the LORD than to put confidence in princes.
—Psalm 118:9

Lincoln's Legacy

Shortly before he was assassinated, President Abraham Lincoln was asked what he would like written on his tombstone.

Lincoln thought and replied, "Whenever I found a thistle, I plucked it and planted a flower in its place."

Blessed are the peacemakers: for they shall be called the children of God. —Matthew 5:9

SOURCES

Introduction

William Safire, *Before the Fall: An Inside View of the Pre-Watergate White House* (New Brunswick, N.J.: Transaction Publishers, 2005).

Walter Isaacson, *Benjamin Franklin: An American Life* (New York: Simon & Schuster, 2003).

Martin Gilbert, *Never Despair: Winston S. Churchill, 1945–1965* (London: Heinemann, 1988).

Stanton Stands Up

Alma Lutz, *Created Equal: A Biography of Elizabeth Cady Stanton, 1815–1902* (New York: Octagon Books, 1974).

Hammarskjöld's Highway

Dag Hammarskjöld, *Markings* (New York: Vintage Books, 2006).

A Red-blooded Hero

Spensie Love, *One Blood: The Death and Resurrection of Charles R. Drew* (Chapel Hill: The University of North Carolina Press, 1996).

Old Master

Grandma Moses, *Grandma Moses, American Primitive; 40 Paintings with Comments by Grandma Moses, together with Her Life's History* (Garden City, N.Y.: Doubleday, 1947).

The Preacher Inspires a President

Philip B. Kunhardt Jr., *A New Birth of Freedom: Lincoln at Gettysburg* (Boston: Little, Brown, 1983).

SOURCES

A Woman Named George
George Eliot, *Janet's Repentance* (New York: G. Munro, 1886).

The Compass of Columbus
Michael Collins, *Carrying the Fire: An Astronaut's Journeys* (New York: Cooper Square Press, 2001).
Felipe Fernández-Armesto, *Columbus* (New York: Oxford University Press, 1991).

The Mexican Lincoln
Nina Brown Baker, *Juarez: Hero of Mexico* (St. Louis: Webster, 1949).

Beauty in the Eye of the Beholder
Edmund Fuller, ed., *2,500 Anecdotes for All Occasions* (New York: Wings Books, 1990), 115.

The Big Little Woman
Alexander K. McClure, *"Abe" Lincoln's Yarns and Stories* (Chicago, 1904).

Word of God
Brian Moynahan, *God's Bestseller: William Tyndale, Thomas More, and the Writing of the English Bible—a Story of Martyrdom and Betrayal* (New York: St. Martin's Press, 2003).

Woomy
William Manchester, *The Last Lion, Winston Spencer Churchill* (Boston: Little, Brown, 1983–1988).

No Time Like the Present
Carl Carmer, *The Susquehanna* (New York: Rinehart, 1955).

Sources

Sharing the Wealth

Edmund Fuller, ed., *2,500 Anecdotes for All Occasions* (New York: Wings Books, 1990), 362.

Latimer's Light

Bergen Evans, ed., *Dictionary of Quotations* (New York: Avenel Books, 1968), 116.

The Gospel According to Another Mark

Ken Hechler, *Working with Truman: A Personal Memoir of the White House Years* (New York: Putnam, 1982).

The Wings of Victory

Kay Halle, ed., *The Irrepressible Churchill: Stories, Sayings, and Impressions of Sir Winston Churchill* (New York: Facts on File Publications, 1985).

Earth Angel

David McCullough, *The Johnstown Flood* (New York: Simon & Schuster, 2004).

Dr. Billy and the Bible

Billy Graham, *Just as I Am: The Autobiography of Billy Graham* (Grand Rapids: Zondervan, 1997).

Good Queen Bess

Alison Weir, *The Life of Elizabeth I* (New York: Ballantine, 1998).

No Fair-weather Friend

Robert H. Ferrell, *Truman, a Centenary Remembrance* (New York: Viking Press, 1984).

Topic Index

Topic Index

Name Index

Scripture Index

Scripture Index